Microsoft Office 365 User Guide

Harri Rosenhelm

Contents

CHAPTER ONE

About Microsoft Office

Microsoft Office 365 is a series of cloud-based productivity and business services. Office 365 is the most comprehensive Office product ever from Microsoft, and combines a cloud-based platform, an online suite of cloud-based applications and Office desktop apps that allow you to take your work everywhere and access it from anywhere. You can even synchronize work between multiple computers.

With Microsoft Office 365, you can access your files from any internet-connected device and collaborate on projects more efficiently. Easily share content with colleagues and clients using OneDrive and OneNote.

Microsoft office 365 is a cloud-based version of the Microsoft office suite. It offers you with a bunch of different tools that are essential for everyday life at work and home. It will enable you to work in real time. The most important part about it is that it works on any PC.

You will get a variety of different tools that are essential for the day- to-day use of Microsoft office 365, such as, Word, Excel, PowerPoint, Outlook, OneNote, Publisher and much more. So that means you will have access to all those things without having to download them to your PC. You can open it on any device. The great thing about Microsoft office 365 is that it offers a bunch of new features. This will help you in different ways.

It is an excellent alternative to traditional Microsoft office programs. You do not have to worry about the security, so you can use all the documents without being worried about viruses and malware.

As you can see, it is a web application that can be accessed by all the devices in the modern world. You will not need to have any software or any files for the activation of the service.

You will need an internet connection, and you can work with your data without having to worry about the access. It gives you the freedom to access your data from anywhere in the world. You can use any browser to access the Microsoft office 365 and your work. It will be a lot easier for you to collaborate and collaborate in groups on any document.

You can use Office 365 after setting it up, and you will need to create your email id. Once you have created the id, you can start working and using it. You will need to choose your security features and the

payment options. After that, you will be able to login to your office 365 account. You can be online in one place and all your files will be available in your account. You can access your files from anywhere. So it will be easier for you to do any work online.

Plan comparison

Organizations and individuals will differ in what they need from Office 365 and that is why there are three plans to choose from. Each plan includes different numbers of applications and features. All the plans are provided for personal use; however, the monthly and yearly plans are also available for organizations. In this book, we will be talking about each of the plans and their specific features.

Free plan

The Free plan is the first plan in the set. It is the lowest priced option and gives you the access to the following applications:

Exchange OneDrive Word Outlook Teams

Visio

Exchange

This plan allows you to use online email services and email on up to 5 devices. There are also some other features such as Exchange ActiveSync, OneDrive, and Outlook.

Office 365 Personal

The Office 365 Personal plan is the second plan and is available for individuals. This plan comes with the option of receiving support and the opportunity to purchase custom licenses for the other plans. It includes access to some applications. This plan allows you to use online email services and email on up to 5 devices.

Office 365 University

The Office 365 University plan is the third plan and is only available for organizations. This plan comes with support and an enterprise license that allows you to use the applications included in the Professional plan. This plan allows you to use online email services and email on up to 5 devices. There are also some other features such as Exchange ActiveSync, OneDrive, and Outlook.

How To Create and Manage a New Microsoft

Office 365 Account

The new Microsoft office 365 account will be required for use in your newly purchased computer and internet connection. So, it's better to create it with Office 365 account. Before that, you must have an active subscription for an account. Therefore, it's important to create the account with the help of online mode.

Before creating a new office 365 account, you need to visit offic e.com/setup/home. Enter the same in the official site. It's better to download office as a zip file. Open the file and then install it on your PC. After that, login to your current Microsoft account. In that case, you will get a login page for your office 365 account.

Steps to create office 365 account

Open a new browser tab, navigate to office.com/setup/home. There are many steps to go to the official site.

Step 1:

After the successful login, you will see the next page. There, you need to press the "Get started" button.

Step 2:

Enter your Windows 10 username and your password. After that, click on the "Next" button.

Step 3:

It's very important to enter the right email address. Don't miss this step. Type the email address which is used for your current Microsoft account.

Step 4:

Now, enter the full name of your Microsoft account and then the last name of your account. Click on the 'Next' button.

Step 5:

Enter your phone number and the last name on the next page. Click on the Next button.

Step 6:

There are two options on the next page. Now, you have to choose the account type. Either you select the free account or you opt for the premium account. Click on the Next button to start the process.

Step 7:

This process will take up to 3-5 minutes. Wait till you see the login success message.

Step 8:

When you'll be done with that, you will see the Login success message on the top.

Step 9:

Congratulations!

The very first thing you need to do is to log in. Just go to your email account in the browser and sign in with the sign-in box.

Step 10:

There is another way. On the very next page, you will be given a password link. Just click on the link and it will guide you through the process to create another sign-in box.

Step 11:

Now, make sure to keep the new password as safe as the old password. Change the settings as per your choice.

Step 12:

And you are done.

How To Install It

To install Microsoft office 365 on your new PC, you must have following two things-

Microsoft Office Home & Student 2020 (latest edition) or Microsoft Office 2019 (latest edition) which is available for Microsoft Home users only.

For Office 365 users, they must have Office 365 Home or Office 365 Student, which is a subscription of Office 365.

1. Download Microsoft office 365

Download Office 365 if you are using Home edition, and if you are using student edition, download Office 365 Student

Download Office 365 Student and Office 365 Home by downloading the respective edition from the official website.

1. Install Microsoft office 365

If you have downloaded the correct version of office 365, then it's time to install it on your PC. Open the Office Setup and click on Install Office 365. Then, you must choose your preferred language from the list and wait for the installation to complete.

1. Configure office 365

After completing the installation of office 365, it's time to configure it. This process will allow you to set your personal preferences and user profile. Once the configuration completes, your Windows 10 installation will be ready.

Now, you have to add an Office 365 account to your new PC.

1. Add a Microsoft office 365 account

Now, you have to add an Office 365 account to your new PC. Enter the following command in the command prompt and provide the required credentials office365.com username password

If you are unable to create your own account in Office 365, then you can select any other free Microsoft account in which you already have an existing username and password.

Microsoft account Username: Enter your Microsoft account username

Office 365 Password: Enter the Office 365 Password

1. Activate Office 365

After completing the configuration process, it's time to activate your Office 365.

Open the Office 365 web portal from your Windows 10 PC.

Click on the 'Sign in' link and enter the password to activate your office 365 subscription.

It will automatically activate your office 365 account and you will be able to use the software and manage your account from the Office 365 home page.

1. Install office apps

Now, you have to install the apps that are required to use Office 365 like Outlook, Word, PowerPoint and OneNote.

Open the Office 365 portal and click on the "App for Windows" link.

Then, you have to choose your language (English, French, German and Italian) and type your username.

After entering your username, search for the app that you want to install. Click on the Install button to install the app.

After the installation, you can click on the App button in the taskbar and get started using the apps.

Benefits Of Microsoft Office

This is the best option for people who have to use Office 365 for personal purposes.

The most suitable office plans available for you to download on your devices is available with Office 365. It is not just a file sharing platform; it provides all the required software that will help you work in the most effective way.

Easy to use. You just have to sign up and then access all the benefits that the plan offers.

Security. All the data that you store is encrypted so that no- one can read or access your data.

Flexibility. You can use all the applications you want. Even if you have a plan with Office 365 but want to use some other applications, you can.

User friendly. The most commonly used applications are well designed so that anyone can use them and make the most out of them.

Increase your productivity and efficiency. More affordable.

Reduce paper use, improve quality and track work Easy online backup for your files.

Save money and energy by connecting to energy-efficient PCs.

Get the benefits of a cloud-based system, including secure online storage and powerful collaborative features.

Access, share and collaborate on documents from any device.

CHAPTER TWO

Apps That Comes With Microsoft Office

Outlook

Outlook on Microsoft office 365 is the perfect solution for those who like to work from anywhere, without compromising on their privacy and security.

You get the advantage of having access to multiple email accounts in a single inbox and access to your work calendar and personal information from anywhere. A unified inbox means you see messages from multiple sources and contacts in one place. Outlook on Microsoft office 365 works like any other version of Microsoft Outlook that is already installed on your device. You can download and use the latest version of Outlook on Microsoft office 365 from the app store of your device.

You can add up to 6 email accounts and you can access your email and your personal calendar from any device. You can also sync your calendar with mobile devices or other services. You can use these features:

Create reminders

Send and receive emails

View all the email you receive from your friends, family and colleagues

Make and receive calls Search for emails

Attach and create documents Create multiple calendars

View your contacts Write and send emails

See your inbox and outbox

Access files online and offline Organize contacts

Track appointments and to-do's Create events

Share, print and archive emails

Read and respond to emails Access and schedule tasks Get email notifications

Outlook on Microsoft office 365 allows you to synchronize your emails, personal calendar, notes and files on your device to your online mailbox. So if you travel or work from anyplace, the information on your device is available to you. You don't have to carry or install the software.

If you find it difficult to travel and work from anyplace, you can use Microsoft Office 365 with Outlook to stay in touch with your friends, family and colleagues. You can use your mobile phone or tablet to work and you can always access your data from any device. All you need is your Microsoft email account.

OneDrive

OneDrive is the cloud-based service of Microsoft. It is a storage area for you to get all the information on your Windows and also a space where you can store other valuable information, like files, and also for sharing.

When you login to your OneDrive account on Windows, the folders automatically get created. These folders are the way you can access the various documents or files stored. The storage capacity for OneDrive can be accessed online and it can be used across Windows 8 and Windows 7, Mac and Mobile Phones, Windows Phone, and even the web. You can upload any of your files or folders to your OneDrive account.

It also acts as a platform for you to share files. With this feature, you can share your files with others, via email, or by sending a link to your files. You can always login to your OneDrive account to access and manage all the files stored there.

Sharepoint

SharePoint is another useful service of Microsoft Office 365, which is a platform to work with your data and also share it with others. This service is free. It can be used by individuals, business owners, schools, and government organizations to store and share their data.

With SharePoint, you can create a web page, build a document, create a PowerPoint presentation, and more.

These pages, presentations and documents can be accessed from the web and from your various devices.

PowerPoint

Presentation files are the basic unit of a digital presentation. PowerPoint is Microsoft's desktop productivity application suite in Microsoft Office 365. You can use PowerPoint for several purposes, such as creating, edit, share, format, print, and convert. We can use the applications as follows, PowerPoint for Office 365, Office PowerPoint, Online PowerPoint, Excel Office 365, PowerPoint in Office 365, and Microsoft PowerPoint Online for Office 365.

PowerPoint can be used for a wide variety of presentations and activities. For example, PowerPoint is used for creating charts, graphs, and images. We can use it to create an interactive web presentation. We can also use PowerPoint for creating educational and training materials. You can save presentation files in PPT format or PPTX format. PowerPoint presentation files can be used to display documents, graphs, or slides and can be embedded in websites, social media, or email, as well as exported as a PDF file.

Format–You can add images, logos, text, and tables.

Slides–You can add multiple slide backgrounds, text, objects, images, and hyperlinks.

Images–You can add multiple images and create custom shapes.

Charts–You can create line graphs, bar graphs, and pie charts.

Animations–You can add various animations to slideshow like fade in/out, text effects, motion graphics, and video effects.

Audio–You can add audio files to your slides, make PowerPoint read a text out loud, and add voiceovers.

SmartArt–You can add tables, charts, shapes, and arrows and shape style graphs.

Document–You can create new presentations, and add and remove various objects from the slides, including images, shapes, text boxes, tables, and media.

Animations–You can add animations to slide objects and create slide transitions to make the slides seem more dynamic.

Templates–You can choose from hundreds of templates to give your presentations a professional look.

Slideshows–You can add effects like fades, motion graphics, and video effects to your slides.

Image gallery–You can insert various image galleries from Bing, Flickr, and the web.

Media gallery–You can insert movies, audio, and other media from either your computer or the web.

Notes–You can add notes to the slides for your presentations or lecture notes.

Links–You can add links to your documents or web pages.
Maps–You can insert maps from Bing, or Google Maps.

Surveys–You can create questionnaires or surveys.

Presenter View–You can choose from a number of pre- created templates to quickly present your content and create a dynamic and unique presentation.

How Mails is used

In general terms, Mails comes with 4 folders: Inbox, Outbox, Drafts, and Sent items. We will show you how we are using Mails in the Sent items folder in this guide;

Let's start with the Inbox, Outbox, and Drafts folders.

If you are using Microsoft Outlook, your Inbox is where all the emails which are being sorted for you will go to. You can also find a couple of useful actions such as mark as read, flag for spam, or move it into a folder, if necessary.

Likewise, the Outbox is where emails are stored for your replies.

Drafts is where you store draft emails that are yet to be sent, however if they get sent, the emails are moved from your Inbox to your Sent items folder. Microsoft have implemented Mails in their Office 365, which enables you to see all the emails that have been sent to you, and received by you.

Calendar

In Microsoft Office 365 Calendar app, the Calendar web app that runs in your browser, there are three types of calendars: Calendars, Scheduling calendars and Shared calendars.

A Calendars store the information of your personal Office 365 account. When you create a new Calendar item, you only need to type the name of the calendar. You can store any type of information in the Calendar. You can also sync the Calendar with your phone so that you have the same information in both your phone and your calendar. When you are using the Calendar in your phone, all your events, and appointments will also be displayed. You can also use your phone to create new calendar items. You can also share your Calendar with your colleagues, so they also have access to your Calendar. This way, they can create new calendar items as well as send reminders. Your colleagues will have access to your calendar, just as you do. Your colleagues can also view your appointments on their calendar. All the information is displayed in the same way as you have it on your phone or in your web browser. If you have an Office 365 subscription, you can read other people's appointments in their Calendars.

A Scheduling calendar is an appointment service. To create appointments on a Scheduling calendar, you need to fill in all the details of the appointment in your calendar. These details include the name, subject, and start and end time of the appointment.

You will also need to choose a time slot. You will need to save the appointment and share it with others. You can also use the mobile app to view your appointments and manage them.

A Shared calendar is where you can invite others to join a Calendar. You can invite others through a link that is sent in an email or by giving them a link on your phone. When you share a calendar, you get a link to that calendar and it looks like an invitation to join. If the recipient of the invitation clicks on it, they will see the calendar and they can also add their own appointments on the calendar.

A Personal calendar is where you can create your own appointments. You can either create events on your own calendar by using the Calendar app. Or you can create and add new events to a public shared calendar. This means that other people can join that shared calendar and see the events that have created.

Calendar events are appointments that you create. These are either private, public, or shared. You can also choose to invite other people to the event. Once the event is created, you can share it with your friends, family, and colleagues. You can also decide to hide the event. If the event is not displayed, it means that it is hidden.

Skype

Microsoft Skype For Business enables collaboration across meetings, video calls, chats, sharing files, and much more for businesses to grow and run efficiently. It lets you create a video- calling bridge between Office 365 and Skype that seamlessly integrates contacts and calendars. Skype in Microsoft Office 365 is designed to enhance your meetings and communication at scale.

Skype in Microsoft Office 365 gives you the flexibility to choose from a range of different ways to participate in a meeting. You can host a meeting, conduct a video call, create a web conference, or collaborate on documents, or any combination of the four. You can choose to join a meeting from your calendar, Skype, or with the click of a button in Outlook on your device. When you're choosing a mode for a meeting, it doesn't matter where you meet. You can start a meeting in Outlook on your mobile device, Outlook on your desktop, Skype on your desktop, or Skype on your mobile device. To set up Skype in Office 365 for your business:

Make sure that all devices that might be used for the meeting are connected to the same Wi-Fi network

You can host a meeting and conduct a video call by using Skype in Office 365. You can also use the Skype for Business Meeting app, Microsoft Teams, Skype in your web browser, or Skype in your mobile device.

When you set up Skype in Office 365, you have different options for a meeting. For example, you can invite people to the meeting when they sign into the Skype in Office 365 app or when they sign into Outlook on their mobile device. You can also create meeting attendees by using Skype in your web browser.

If you're using Microsoft Teams, you have two options for a meeting. In Teams, you can create a new team project, invite people to a meeting by using the Skype in Office 365 app, or use the online meeting tool in your web browser.

If you have a meeting scheduled on Skype for Business, you can start the meeting by clicking the meeting icon in your calendar. You can also set the meeting location and options for the meeting before you start the meeting.

You can start a meeting on Skype in Office 365 by clicking the Meeting icon on your calendar. The calendar includes the options for a meeting, such as when the meeting starts and ends, the meeting title, and the locations for the meeting.

When you invite people to Skype in Office 365 meeting, you can choose to join the meeting using the Skype in Office 365 app or by using your phone or computer.

If you're inviting people to a meeting, click "Start Meeting" to start the meeting. You can also click the calendar button to start a meeting immediately, or click a button that says "Start as Web Meeting" to set the meeting up so that it starts in your web browser.

When you invite people to a meeting by using your phone or computer, you can click "Invite By Phone" or "Invite By Email."

When you invite people to a meeting by clicking "Invite By Phone" or "Invite By Email," you might need to choose the phone number or email address. You can select it on the "Select Your Invitation" screen of your Skype for Business app. (For more information, see "Add phone numbers and email addresses to your Skype for Business contacts' list".)

When you invite people to a meeting, you can also invite them by sending them a link to a Skype for Business meeting invitation. (For more information, see "Start meetings in Skype for Business from a link.")

You can end a meeting by clicking the Meeting button on your calendar. You might need to click the calendar button to display the calendar. Then, click the Meeting button to open a meeting window. From the Calendar window, click 'End' to end the meeting. If you start a meeting with the Web Client, you can close the meeting by clicking the meeting's button in the navigation bar.

Excel

Microsoft Excel is one of the most popular and commonly used software of Microsoft. It is not just used in business, but also used in different areas like social media, sports, education, retail, politics, and many others. In 2019, over 70% of all computers had at least one version of Excel installed in them.

Excel supports multiple file formats like TXT, CSV, XLSX, and many others. It is one of the most user-friendly software tools to handle data. With the introduction of Microsoft 365, Excel is the integral part of that. Microsoft Excel is known to be a part of Microsoft Office 365 subscription plans.

Now, the basic features of Microsoft Excel are the same as in the standalone version.

The difference is that Excel is a part of an Office 365 subscription that includes the use of a number of other Microsoft products.

We have to admit that Excel, as a single tool, is a lot more than we have covered here.

The basic features of Excel make it the best database software.

It can be used to manage information and create data that can be used for analysis and reporting.

It has the features like conditional formatting, charts, data tables, calculation, pivot tables, and more.

Data can be stored in a variety of data formats like Excel, PDF, SQL, XML, CSV, and many others.

Excel allows the user to create spreadsheets in several file formats, like CSV, XLS, TXT, and HTML.

An Excel spreadsheet allows adding multiple sheets to a single document.

Excel allows us to sort data on different criteria and can be sorted on various columns.

Excel enables one to create conditional formats in it which enable you to format different portions of the spreadsheet depending on the values in it.

OneNote

OneNote is a very good Microsoft word processor. You can easily use it as a normal word processor. OneNote works well for collaborative writing and note-taking. The only problem is that you cannot make good OneNote documents for a normal Microsoft word processor. You cannot just drag-and-drop images, text boxes or tables on it. To put those things on OneNote, you need to use Microsoft office 365. That's the whole story. You need to install Microsoft office 365 to be able to make a good OneNote document on a normal Microsoft word processor. On the contrary, you can save your word processing documents to OneNote on a normal Microsoft word processor. All these are the benefits that you will get from using the Microsoft word editor.

1. Create notes

You can create notes just like you would in any other Microsoft application. Just open the Microsoft application that you are working in, type your note in the note book, save it and it will be synced to your OneNote online.

1. Add shapes, animations, photos, audio

OneNote allows you to insert images, movies, animations, sound clips and much more in your notes.

To add images to your note, you can use the clip art viewer or upload your own images. With oneNote, you can also add text boxes, text and shapes to your notes.

To add an audio clip or a sound clip, just upload a clip of your voice to your OneNote account. That way, all your notes will sync to your oneNote.

1. Add links

OneNote supports links. Links: take you to a web page, a document, your outlook mail, a social network or anywhere else on the web.

You can use OneNote's built-in web browser to open links or you can right click on the link to open it directly in a browser.

1. Connect to services

You can connect OneNote to the apps you use. When you insert a URL in OneNote, it opens in the connected application and adds a hyperlink to it.

1. Share

In OneNote, it's super easy to share your notes.

Right click on the note you want to share and click share. Choose which apps you want to share it with and with which level of access.

OneNote is truly a powerful note-taking app.

CHAPTER THREE

How To Set Up Office and SharePoint

Go to your office account > select the app. Select settings on the app.

Scroll down and select SharePoint.

You will be asked to select whether you want to connect your Microsoft 365 account to the SharePoint account and the type of organization you are part of. Choose the desired option.

Click the sign-in button.

You are now in the Microsoft Office 365 Portal. Here you will be able to set the username and password for the SharePoint account. Also, you can change the account admin password. If you are part of a global company, you can also add different members to different groups. You can also set the default folders and settings that your Office apps can use.

After completing all the settings, click on the next step.

You will now be on the "Choose apps to install" screen. Here you can select apps like Excel, Word, PowerPoint and Outlook.

Click on the "Install" button on the top right to start the installation process.

After the apps installation completes, your Office 365 SharePoint applications will be ready.

How To Set Up OneDrive for Business

Step 1: Sign in to your Office 365 account Log in to your Office 365 account

Step 2: Click the gear icon on the top right of your screen.

Step 3: On the 'Settings' section, click 'Apps'

Step 4: Here, you can see the currently installed apps. Check out the 'OneDrive' app to get started.

Step 5: Click the '+' icon on the right side. You will be asked to select the apps which you wish to install. Select the 'OneDrive for business app, and click on 'Install'.

Step 6: Once it is installed, you will get a small notification, saying that 'OneDrive for business' has been successfully installed.

Step 7: You can use it to access and edit your files from anywhere.

OneDrive for business is an additional app you can install in your Office 365 account. All the above steps explained how to install, configure and use OneDrive for business for a regular user. For a business user, it is even simpler to get started. The steps are much simpler, as you just need to follow the instructions for business users in the previous steps.

CHAPTER FOUR

How To Set Up Stream

Step 1: Create a Microsoft account for the Office 365 experience, and log into it using the Account Settings page. Go to the Office 365 settings on your account and navigate to Online Services & Applications. Click on Additional Services and scroll to Office 365, and click Turn On Office 365 Services.

Step 2: After successful sign in, you should be redirected to the main page of Office 365 Admin. Go to Your Apps on the left side navigation and scroll down to find the Stream tab. Click on it.

Step 3: From there, you can sign up for the trials and start working with the service.

Note: For this experience, you don't need to have Microsoft account set up on your PC.

How To Use Video Conferencing

Video conferencing in Microsoft office 365 is not new. But with Microsoft's new additions, there is a huge change in video conferencing application. It is much faster, smoother, and seamless. Let's see how to do it.

Step 1: First, you need to be logged into Microsoft Online services.

Step 2: After that, open Microsoft Office365 portal and open Outlook.com. Click on the mail icon and click on the "inbox". Then click on "New email".

Step 3: Then click on "Join a meeting" After that, you will be taken to the video conferencing screen. You will also see an option, "Video conferencing".

Step 4: If you click on that, you will be taken to the video conferencing screen. The screen will open up and look like a new window. You will see the list of people, from that you can select the person you wish to talk with. After that you need to press "Begin". It will automatically start to record and video call with your selected person.

You can also start the video conference in this way too. If someone is invited and want to join, first, he will be asked to accept the invite and second, he will be redirected to a page where he will have to accept or decline the invite.

You can also decline the request to join the call and not participate. It will show you in a notification that you have been declined.

You can click on the notification and in the drop-down menu, select "join". It will redirect you to a page where you can join the video conference.

How To Change The Name Of A Document

In Microsoft office 365, you can't change the name of your documents as such. If you want to change the name of your documents, it should be done within the same document set.

Step 1: Start Microsoft Office 365.

Step 2: Click on Documents.

Step 3: Click on the name of the document set.

Step 4: Click on Rename.

Step 5: You'll be prompted to log in. Enter your username and password.

Step 6: Enter the name for the document set.

Step 7: Click on the OK button.

Go back to your document set and the new name will be applied.

How To Join A Meeting

To join a meeting, you need to follow a few simple steps:

1. Join meeting

This will bring you to the meeting invite. If you have already been invited to the meeting and you want to join in, then you don't need to log in. The meeting will already be open for you.

Note: You need to give permission to join the meeting.

Step 1: To join a meeting, select the meeting you are interested in from the list.

Step 2: Once you have selected the meeting, you will be able to join in.

1. Start meeting

In the upper right corner of the meeting room, you will see a start button. Click on it to join the meeting. You will be able to join in the meeting right away. If you are given the ability to join the meeting, select start from the list and join in.

Note: Do you want to join a Microsoft Power BI meeting? Click on the Meeting link and select the Meeting start button. Click on start to join.

Join a meeting by clicking on the meeting link, select the meeting name and start meeting from the list.

Step 1: Select the meeting you are interested in from the list.

Step 2: The second page will list the topics being discussed in the meeting. You can choose the topic or not.

Step 3: Click on the start button to start the meeting.

If you have already been invited to the meeting, you will be able to join in the meeting right away.

1. See previous meetings

In the upper right corner of the meeting room, you will see a calendar button. Click on it to see previous meetings that you have participated in. You will be able to see the list of all your previous meetings.

How To End A Meeting

Step 1: Open Outlook

If you don't have Outlook, you can download the latest version of Outlook for PC or Mac.

Step 2: Go to Calendar view

Now, click on the Calendar icon at the top right corner to view your calendar.

Step 3: Go to the Meetings tab

On the calendar view, click on the Meetings tab.

Step 4: Find the meeting you want to end and then click the x icon (cross)

At the end of the meeting, click on the x icon (cross) in the meeting to end the meeting.

Method 2: End a meeting in MS office 365 Using Google calendar

You can also use Google calendar to end a meeting. Just follow these steps to end a meeting in office 365.

Step 1: Open Google Calendar

If you don't have a Google account, create an account.

Step 2: Go to calendar view

Now, click on the calendar icon at the top right corner.

Step 3: Go to the Meetings tab

On the calendar view, click on the Meetings tab.

Step 4: Find the meeting you want to end and then click the x icon (cross)

At the end of the meeting, click on the x icon (cross) in the meeting to end the meeting.

CHAPTER FIVE

How To Create and Send a Document

Step 1: Go to File–> New–> Document

Step 2: Select a File–> Browse for the file

Step 3: Select the location of the file where you want to create the document

Step 4: Click on Open

Step 5: Set the name of the document and click on Finish Step 6: Open Microsoft office and select the company file. Step 7: Select the name of the company.

Step 8: Set the visibility to Public

Step 9: Open the document in Microsoft office 365. You will be able to see the file in your documents.

Step 10: Click on Files in the top right-hand corner of the screen.

Step 11: Go to File–> Share

Step 12: Click on the check box “Allow only approved recipients to see this document.”

Step 13: Select the name of the person who has to receive the document

Step 14: Click on OK

Step 15: You will see a confirmation dialog box. Confirm and click on OK.

Step 16: You will see a dialog box which says “Send Successful”

Step 17: Now the recipient will receive a message that he will receive a message with the file

The above steps will guide you in sharing documents in office 365. Follow the same steps for a different folder and you can share the folder in office 365.

How To Save A Document

Select the document you wish to save Open the File menu and click on Save As.

You may choose any location in which you wish to save the file. The document you are currently viewing will be listed on the left pane.

How to Attach Documents In An Email

Go to Outlook > click File > Add Attachment > Add File Select the desired files.

Choose an attachment format (e.g., Word | PDF)

Choose which folder to save the attachment in.

Note that you can choose where you want to save these attachments instead of saving them to the same folder that you've been emailing from.

To open the attachments: Click the Email icon

Click the Attachments tab Drag & Drop

Select the file you wish to open

Different Kinds of Words Styles

Bullet points: used in a list

Text: standard text

Italics: used in a quote or to highlight something

Emphasis: used in a quote or to highlight something

Superscript: a single number that is above the standard text

Subscript: a single number that is below the standard text

Small caps: used for title names in MS office 365 and other Microsoft products

Bold: used to highlight text and titles in MS office 365 and other Microsoft products

How To Create A New Word Style

Right click on the word, choose Insert - Normal. Under the 'Symbol' tab, select the new style you want.

How To Highlight A Text

You can find it on the menu, or you can use CTRL+SHIFT+A to toggle it. (or CTRL+SHIFT+U)

Go to Word > Home > Style > Highlighting. You will see an option in the highlight properties to enable "Text Highlighting"

OR

In PowerPoint:

Select the text.

Press the Ctrl+Spacebar to show the “highlighting pane”. Click the “Font” menu item.

Select “Font Group” to make a new group.

Now select all the text in the highlighted pane. From the menu you will see the “Font group menu”.

To make the Highlight appear on PowerPoint, Select the text you want to highlight.

Click on the Home tab, then on the Format menu, then on the Highlight tab.

Choose a text color and a color fill.

CHAPTER SIX

How To Set Up PowerPoint

Step 1. Connect your office 365 with a stable internet and login in to your office 365.

Step 2. Click on the Office Apps for your computer.

Step 3. You will be able to see two different windows. In this step, you can install both the office 365 desktop and online apps.

Step 4. Click on the Desktop to install the PowerPoint on your PC.

Step 5. Now you need to select the language and then select the option to add PowerPoint to the list of Office 365 Apps. You need to click on the button Install now.

Step 6. Now, go to the control panel. In this step, you can set the screen resolutions, change the color, etc.

Step 7. After that, you can also save the changes, change the security, privacy and other important settings. After these settings, you need to click on save and close to save the changes.

Step 8. Now, you need to start the installation process, go to the Control panel and select the option which says "Start Installation." In this step, click on Install.

Step 9. You can download the PowerPoint app from the Office website and then click on install it. Now, you need to select the language, then select the option to install the PowerPoint app.

Step 10. After that, you need to select the file name, location and then click on Install now. Now, your PowerPoint is set up on the office 365 PC.

How To Create a PowerPoint Presentation

SignintoyourOffice365account: https://my.office.com/#home/user and click "Sign in".

Select "Sign in to your Microsoft 365 account" and login to your Office 365 account.

Now click on the "PowerPoint icon" found at the top right- hand corner.

On the next screen, click on "Add New".

On the next screen, click on "Create your presentation".

Now you will be able to create a new presentation. On the next screen, click on "Save".

A box appears on the left-hand side. This box contains all the options required for the PowerPoint. Click on "Insert".

On the next screen, you will find a PowerPoint icon. Click on the PowerPoint icon.

How To Make Slide and Add Picture

The "Insert slide" menu will appear on the top right-hand corner of the window. Now you can start making a presentation. A new screen appears on the right-hand side. Now you can start adding images, documents, etc.

It is recommended to add the background picture. On the next screen, you can select different types of shapes.

You can add a slide with text on the top. For this, you need to add the title.

Click on the "+" icon. A new text box will appear. Type your title.

Now you can add a different kind of slides. Click on the "+" icon. This screen will let you select different shapes to add. To add shapes, click on the "+" icon.

How to Create Animated Videos In PowerPoint

You can add videos. To add videos, first you need to download them.

Now, click on the "+" icon. Click on "Videos". Now select the video you want to add to the presentation.

You can select different formats. It can be MPEG, AVI, WMV, MP4, etc. Now, you can add different effects and transitions. You can add different transitions as well.

Select the transition you want to add to the video. You can also select "Fade".

This page will help you edit the title of the slide. You can change the fonts and colors. You can add a background. You can add the image in full-screen mode. You can also adjust the brightness, contrast, and zoom.

Click on the "+" icon to add more slides. You can add as many slides as you like. Now you can add different texts to the slide. You can customize the fonts, styles, and colors.

Click on the "+" icon to add your own background image. You can choose different styles for the background. You can select background images from your device or from Google.

Now you can customize different aspects of your presentation.

CHAPTER SEVEN

How To Set Up Email

On the left-hand side of the screen, click on Mail and click on "settings" and select "mail accounts".

Next, click the Add button.

Select "New email account" from the menu.

Enter a name for your new account. You may choose a different account name on the next screen.

Enter your username and password. Click Save to save your new account.

Next, Sign-in to your new account by clicking on the Sign In link at the top of the screen.

Type your username and password you selected in the previous step.

Once you have signed in, you can click on the e-mail box to the left of your name.

How To Use The Email Services

When you first open your Office 365 mail in Outlook, you will see a Welcome screen. You can get to the actual e-mail list by clicking on Settings from the bottom-right corner of the screen.

You can click on Options and change the way that the mail list shows up. One of the options is to show it as a list or as an app. The list view is similar to the Microsoft Outlook list view, but the app view is a more modern version.

The main purpose of Microsoft Office 365 Mail is to keep your e-mail messages in the OneDrive cloud, just like you would with Outlook on a desktop. You can read your messages from anywhere that has Internet access.

There is also a button on your mail list that says Open with OneNote. When you click on this button, you can open all of your e-mails in OneNote. This is an online word processing program that has special features, like drawing. OneNote also comes with the Office 365 apps on the phone and tablet, and if you have an Office 365 subscription, you can access your Microsoft Office documents on the web without a download.

When you get a new message, there is a button that says Send as Mail. This works like a mail client that creates a Microsoft Exchange folder with the message attached. You can then forward it to another e-mail address. You will get an e-mail with a notification to tell you that the mail has been forwarded.

There is also a button that says Send to Outlook.com. When you click on this button, the mail will be sent directly to a Microsoft

Outlook folder in your e-mail.

There is also a link on the bottom of the screen that says Share. When you click on this, a box will pop up, and it has buttons for the e-mail account you are using. The buttons for the others are also there. You can send any of the e-mails you have to them. You will also be able to print and forward the e-mails you are reading.

How To Send Mails to Multiple Recipient

Step 1: Click on New Mail, select your Account and then select Add to Outlook at the bottom.

Step 2: Then click on add e-mail address.

Step 3: Give a name to the email, a comment for future reference (optional) and then add the Email Address in the "To" tab, for this, choose "multiple recipients", then click on "send" (or save).

OR

First, you must configure your email account. Then you can create a new mailbox and add a number of email addresses (to use this add- on, first you must have a Microsoft Office 365 mailbox).

Here is how to do that:

Step 1: Configure your mailbox:

Step 2: On the navigation bar, click on Mail.

Step 3: Click on New mail and select your mailbox.

Step 4: Create a new mailbox. On the left menu bar, click on Mail.

Step 5: Select New. On the Mail box screen, on the left side, click on the Add an email address.

Step 6: Select your mailbox and type your email address, then click on the Add button. Add your email addresses.

On the left menu bar, click on Mail. Select your mailbox.

On the mail box screen, click on the Add an email address.

Select your mailbox and type your email address, then click on the Add button.

If you want to use add-on to manage your mail, click on your mailbox and click on the Manage button.

If you want to add add-on to add or remove contacts, select Contacts on the left and then click on the + button. Add your contacts as described there.

CHAPTER EIGHT

How To Create Forms

Step 1. Open Microsoft office 365 for Desktop.

Step 2. Go to the main screen where you find design tools like drawing tools, tables, charts, images, forms, etc.

Step 3. Click on the Insert form button

Step 4. Click on the Create a form.

Step 5. Select the template type.

Step 6. Click on 'Next' to open the form creation page.

Step 7. Select the place where you want to insert the form. Click on the down arrow button, select the place where you want to insert the form, and click on Add.

Step 8. Once the form is completed,

Step 9. Click on the Create form button.

Step 10. The form is created successfully.

How To Create Charts

Charts are one of the most effective ways to visualize all your data in an organized manner. Microsoft office 365 provides you with some of the best chart tools that you will need to effectively create charts in office 365. There are many chart options for office 365 users to use, but you need to know the right chart tool in office 365 that will suit your needs.

If you don't have any charts tool in your office 365, you might want to first learn how to create charts in office 365. To do that, you need to follow these steps;

Step 1: First, create an empty PowerPoint presentation and name the slide. In this case, we are creating a bar chart.

Step 2: Now open the chart sheet and right click on the area and choose insert > pie or insert > horizontal for making a pie or column chart.

Step 3: Then, select pie chart and from the drop down select your field from your dataset. It must be in your table.

Step 4: Enter the values that you want to show and click OK to create the pie chart.

Step 4: When the pie chart is completed and you hover the mouse over it, a drill down menu appears. You can also click on the pie to see the options.

How To Create Reports

Step 1: First, create a new Excel workbook and name it report.xls (or whatever you want). Now we need to make sure that we're using the correct Excel versions for our report. To do this, go to Excel, click on File and then click on Options, and finally click on the Advanced tab. Now we'll select the latest version of Excel we want to use for the report.

Step 2: You can also make sure you're using the correct version of Excel in Office 365 by clicking the gear button next to Office 2016 (for example) in the Office 365 application and select the Microsoft Office version that you are using. This makes sure that you are using the correct version of Excel.

Step 3: Now, in the Excel, we want to add an existing worksheet to our report. The most obvious way to do this is to simply drag the worksheet that you want to include in the report from the worksheets tab to the report.

The report can now be published. So how do you publish the report?

Step 1: Open Office and from File click on Open. Find the report that you just created. The reports can be found in either the same directory or in a subdirectory.

Step 2: Now click on 'Save As' and save the report as a Microsoft Office word document (.docx). Then save it to the same location as the report. This will be the location on your PC that you'll send it to your stakeholders.

Step 3: Once the document is sent, your stakeholders will be able to edit the document with an XML editor such as word processor or excel.

Step 4: Finally, we want to include a page break. So in Word, click on Insert > Page break. Do the same for Excel.

You can now start the conversation with your stakeholders.

How To Build Graphs

Microsoft team has now come up with a new app called Graph. Microsoft now believes that we should try to organize a lot more information in digital world and not only paper world. With their help, it is now possible to build graphs within any document of word, Excel, etc.

Graphs are needed to:

To give a new perspective to the user

Graph help you to visualize data in an interesting way. You can view any info or any information in any form and in any way. You can make graphs as a bar graph or line graph.

You can also share your graphs with others by just sharing it. Sharing graphs is a great way to help people visualize data.

For research

If you have a research or any task that involves data analysis, making graphs is the best way to help you. Making graphs is also an easy way to create reports and share your work with others.

Graphs can give you insights into any information in the shortest possible way

Gadgetry

With the help of graphs, we can analyze data in a better way To present it easily to the public

If you need to present the data in the way that they understand it.

Graphs are the best way to explain the data. You can also give different presentations of the same data and different colors will help you to see different parts clearly.

How to build graphs?

When you will try to build graphs, you need to go to the Office 365 apps. You have to search for Graph.

Once you are on Graph tab, you will see a list of your favorite graph types.

To add new graph to your favorites, you can click on Add. You will get another screen to add a new graph.

You will get few options to select the color. Finally, select the graph and start using it.

CHAPTER NINE

How To Create Your Own Personal Cloud Storage

These steps will show you how to create your own personal cloud storage in Microsoft office 365. You will be able to backup all your important files to it. It is a really simple process. Just make sure that you have Office 365. If you do not have a premium plan, you can just skip this step. In that case, you will need Office 365 enterprise. You can download a trial version of Office 365 on your computer for a week. For premium version, you have to subscribe. You can have a 30-day trial version of Office 365.

Step 1

Create a new storage site in Microsoft store. Click on "Create storage site."

Select the location where you want to store your files.

Type the name of the new storage site.

Save it with a name that you want.

Step 2

Connect to Office 365 enterprise.

Navigate to your office 365 enterprise account on your account on Office 365.

Click "Create site."

Choose the type of site that you want to create.

Select the storage location that you want to be connected to. Click "Create".

Step 3

Add a folder to the new site.

Go to the storage location where you want to store your files. Click on the site that you have created.

Create a folder on the site.

Step 4

Copy your files to the new storage site.

Select the storage location on the new site. Go to the location where you have your files. Click on the files in your storage location.

Click on “Copy here”.

Step 5

Download the files.

Go to the storage location that you have just created. Click on the files that you have copied.

Click “Download” to download your files.

Step 6

Connect to the new storage site in OneDrive.

To connect to your newly created storage site, go to your online OneDrive account.

Click on your name at the top right of your screen. Go to “File Manager” on the right side of the page. Click on “Storage” in the bottom right of the screen. Select the site where you want to copy your files to. Click “Upload” to transfer your files.

Step 7

Download your files.

After the files are uploaded, go to your storage site in the OneDrive. Click on the files that you have uploaded.

Click on "Download" to download your files.

Tips

You can also create a backup of your files to access them in the event of any file corruption. To do this, go to your storage location, go to "File Manager", and click "Start a new backup." This will add the files to a new folder.

You can access your files from the File Manager without logging in.

If you see an error message saying that you do not have permissions to view the file, then go to the owner of the file, click on "File Manager," and click "Change Permissions." Select the permissions that you want and click "Ok."

Using Pivot Table

What is Pivot table?

A pivot table is a tool that lets you organize and analyze data in a spreadsheet. It displays data in multiple view. We can use a Pivot table in MS Excel for creating reports and analyzing our data. The best thing about pivot table is, you can change the view of the data anytime.

Pivot table is a good way to visualize your data. It is the easiest way to explore your data. We will use a pivot table in office 365, because it is easy to make changes.

How to create Pivot table in office 365

Open the sample excel file you have downloaded. Click on the pivot table.

On the Pivot Table screen, click on the 'New'.

A pop-up window will open.

We now have a blank Pivot table and we will start analyzing our sample data.

Add Columns

You can add any number of columns to your Pivot table to view the data in different ways.

We can add as many columns as we want in our Pivot table.

The column labels do not matter. You can use any label for the columns.

Let's add a new column to show the value.

Add Rows

We can add any number of rows to our Pivot table to show how we want to analyze the data.

Finally

Pivot table is a great way to create a dynamic report to display a data set in the form of a chart. By using a dynamic Pivot table, you can generate a lot of valuable reports quickly.

How To Use The Audio Tool

To access the Audio Tool in Microsoft office 365, click the arrow on the toolbar and then choose Add-Ins > Office Add-Ins > Audio Add- In.

Once the add-in opens, click on the gear icon and then click on "Enable Audio Tool".

The Video tool will appear. To use the Audio tool, click on the Record button in the "Record Audio" section.

You can highlight the audio in your recording with the different colors and click the Stop Record button.

Click the red button on the Stop Recording button, and then you can listen to the audio file you have made.

Note: This tool is only available for Microsoft Office 365 subscribers and not in the Home edition.

There are many ways you can make an audio clip, such as recording audio files, using an audio recorder and using your webcam, and many other ways.

You can have audio files on your computer, or you can record your voice in the microphone, or you can record it from the webcam.

These steps will help you create an audio clip from your voice files. You can also listen to your voice recordings or audio clips by clicking the buttons provided in the "Recording" section.

Step 1: Select the recording tool

Go to the "Record Audio" section and click on the Red record button.

Select "Record audio,"

Step 2: Say something

Say something into the microphone and wait until it beeps. Say something into the microphone

Note: You can play the audio file later by clicking the Play button.

Step 3: Record your voice and listen

Click on the recording file and you can listen to the audio clip that you have made.

What happens if you have Microsoft office 365 subscription and then do you know how to turn on the “Record Audio” section in Microsoft office 365 online? you have to go to the “Settings” tab and select “Recording”.

Go to Settings > Recording and record your voice

Microsoft office 365 subscribers use the Recorder tool daily. The new Recorder tool is a useful tool that allows users to record audio, and then share or download it later.

You can record files like audio, video, or any documents in the Microsoft office 365 online with the help of the Recorder tool. You can record from your browser or microphone, or you can upload files or documents and then save the file for later use.

The Recorder tool also lets you download the files from the Recorder tool as MP3 format audio files or you can upload the files to the cloud storage or any storage.

Using the Recorder tool, you can record documents, videos, voice clips, etc, without the need of downloading and installing any tool.

Let’s now have a look at the steps to record audio files.

Sign in to your account on Microsoft office 365. Click on the “File” option from the menu.

Click on "New", then select the "Voice" option and click on "Record".

Now, you will hear a beep and a message "Please say your message". This is a confirmation that the recording tool is ready to record your message.

Click on "Start Recording" to record your message.

Now the "Record Audio" section will appear, select the "Record Files" option.

Click on "Select Files", choose the files and files you want to record and click on "Record Files".

Now, it will ask for the files to be recorded. In the list, select the files and click on "Record Files".

Once done, you can play back the files that have been recorded.

These are the steps to record audio files. If you are facing any problem while recording your voice, in such a case you can contact the Microsoft technical support. You can either dial the technical support number or send them a mail to the technical support.

How To Backup with OneDrive

Microsoft office 365 brings to the users many additional features, including the OneDrive storage. It's available to all the users who have purchased the MS office 365 subscription, and it's very easy to sync files from other storage to OneDrive, as this software offers a OneDrive sync folder, where you can create sync folders and save files. You can store your photos, videos, office files, etc. in the OneDrive. By doing so, you won't lose your files even if the OneDrive service is not available.

OneDrive is a product of Microsoft, and you will need to use it for backup, to access files in one place. But what if you use another storage? For example, how would you backup your office files from Dropbox or Google Drive?

For this, you have to perform OneDrive backup, and do this in two ways. There are two ways to backup the files to OneDrive:

By creating OneDrive sync folder, By exporting the files.

In these steps, we will learn how to backup office files from DropBox to OneDrive.

Step 1. Create OneDrive sync folder

To backup the files to OneDrive, you have to first create a OneDrive sync folder. To create it, you just have to open

OneDrive in your browser and click on 'Create' and select a folder for the synchronization.

Once you have selected a folder, you will see the files in the dropbox

Click on the sync button on the bottom of the screen, then you will see the files in your OneDrive as well.

Now you will see both OneDrive and Dropbox at the same time, and you can easily copy files from one to the other.

Step 2. Backup Files from Dropbox to OneDrive

Now you have your Dropbox account linked to your OneDrive account. Let's start with the first way to backup your files to OneDrive, by creating a sync folder.

If you already have a OneDrive folder, click on the + sign on the top left corner and choose Select a folder, then click on the Browse button on the bottom left corner.

Enter the name of your folder, and click on Choose Folder. You can enter any name for your folder. Then click on the Open.

Now in your Dropbox, files are selected. You can now copy the files to OneDrive folder by going to Files and then select the OneDrive folder. Now you will see the files in the right-hand corner.

Select the files you want to backup. If you want to upload files from Dropbox to OneDrive, select Files, then Select OneDrive folder, select the file, and click on Choose file.

When the file selection is completed, you will see a Download to OneDrive button.

Click on it and your files will be uploaded to OneDrive.

CHAPTER TEN

How To Create An Event

Step 1: Click on Office 365 from the top menu.

Step 2: On the right-hand side, click on Events from the Office 365 Admin.

Step 3: Click on the New button at the bottom of the menu.

Step 4: Fill in the event details.

Fill in the Event Title, Type (it can be a webinar, meeting, talk or conference), Description, Where, Time, Agenda and attendees.

The Agenda is your most important feature in an event. It's usually in three parts:

- The intro/outro part includes the intro and end of your event. Use this as an introduction or a summary of what you'll be discussing in your event. It can be about one to two minutes long.

- The body includes the talk/expert session. This is where you'd discuss all of your points or questions. Use it to talk about all the points you plan on discussing.
- The last part is the conclusion. At the end of the talk/session, you'll typically have some conclusion or some action items. This is where you'd end your talk/session. Use it to discuss any points you'll be doing.

You can use a slide deck to share your session. Alternatively, you can use Microsoft PowerPoint or other pre-designed presentations and add your content to them.

To add a slide deck, use the File menu and select Import or Choose an existing presentation.

You can share your session by using the Share screen in PowerPoint or the File menu to send it by email or Share by Skype, the Google Drive or Facebook.

You can also add a video by inserting a YouTube link, a Vimeo link, or just by using your webcam.

How To Schedule A Meeting

A meeting in Office 365 is same as a meeting in any other collaboration platform. All you need is a link to that meeting and people will start the meeting by clicking on the link.

For that, you will need a link to that particular meeting. You can get that by following these steps:

Make sure that you are an admin and you can invite people to the meeting. If you don't have the admin level, then you will have to create that level by visiting Office 365 admin center.

Step 1: Go to the group where you want to organize the meeting and click on that group. You will see a heading called group activity.

Step 2: Choose an option that says Add a Group Meeting

Step 3: In the next step, you will see two buttons. One is New Group Meeting, and the other is Link to Meeting. Click on the latter button. It will show a link.

Step 4: Then click on that link and you will be able to see a pop-up where you can click on New Meeting from the below menu,

Step 5: In this window, you will be able to either manually invite people to this meeting, or you can send an invite to someone by clicking on the Invite a person button on the left side of the pop-up. You can send the invites to people in your organization or to external users by selecting External Participants option.

Step 6: Once people click on the Invite button, it will take them to this meeting invitation form. Here is where you can either enter your email address and click on the Send button, or you can send a link to the person who you want to invite as well.

Step 7: After all this, click on the OK button and the people who will get the meeting invitation will see a new invitation on their calendar, with all the details of the meeting as well as the link to that invite. There is a custom invite button if you want to do custom designs for it. But in general, this is how you organize a meeting in Microsoft 365.

How To Invite People For An Event

If you want to invite people to an event, click Invited Guests to open a new window. To invite someone, click their name, and then click Add Guest. A message will appear telling the person that you are adding him/her to the event. When the person accepts the invitation, the added person will be placed in your calendar in the calendar view.

How To Start A Conversation In A Group

First, you need to create a SharePoint online group by navigating to Groups in the left-side navigation pane. If the group is a SharePoint On-Premises Group, the process is similar.

After you created the group, click the cog icon next to the group name and choose the "Add people" button. Enter the names of the people you want to add. You can add as many people as you want.

At this point, you can start the conversation by choosing the green down arrow next to the group name.

When you click the green down arrow, you will see the following process:

After a few moments, a window similar to the following will open: The people in the group are now added to your conversation.

If you want to leave the conversation, click on the arrow next to the

group name again, this time choosing the red up arrow. This will remove the people from your conversation.

Please note that you do not have to add the person to your conversation in a specific order. If you want to add someone who was not part of the conversation yet, you can just click on the green down arrow and type in the name. The person's name will be added to the conversation automatically.

Note: Adding someone as part of your conversation is not an action in the process; the conversation will add and update it automatically.

You do not have to do anything manually for the person to be added as part of the conversation.

Once you removed someone from the conversation, you will have the ability to keep the conversation or close it, and remove the person from your Conversation window.

If you wanted to keep the conversation, you can now do that by clicking on the arrow next to the group's name.

It may take a few moments for the other people in the conversation to see that the person was removed from the conversation and be able to react.

CHAPTER ELEVEN

How To Set Up Excel

Step 1: Now you need to create a new Microsoft Office 365 user for your business.

Step 2: On your desktop go to Start > All programs > Microsoft office

> office 365 > and then click on sign up.

Step 3: When you are on the sign-up page, just sign in with your Microsoft account or your Office 365 account.

Step 4: On the next page, in the username text box, enter your username. In the email text box, enter your email address. On the password text box, enter the same password that you have used while signing into Microsoft office 365. In the password hint, enter a simple hint to help the user remember his password.

Step 5: Click on next, after filling all the required details, enter the Microsoft account, which is used to activate your Microsoft office 365 account.

Step 6: Once you click on 'Create', you will be redirected to your new account dashboard. Here you can manage your subscription and data from Microsoft OneDrive, Microsoft storage, and Office programs. Here you can find more details about how to change your password, add another user account for an employee, add custom services, etc.

Step 7: Now, you need to set up Microsoft Excel 365 on the new user account. This is required because if you are not using the Excel

you would not be able to open the workbook that you already created in Excel. Here we will be using the free version. For more advanced version, you can consider Office 365.

Step 8: Open Excel and sign into the new account.

Step 9: Enter the details and set up the user and the password.

Step 10: Enter your Microsoft account and choose the region that you are in to setup your settings for using Excel 365.

Step 11: Download the Excel 365 from the Office 365 page and install it on your PC.

Step 12: Now enter your password to sign into Excel 365.

Step 13: Once you sign in, the Microsoft account password should automatically be updated.

Step 14: Now you can create a new workbook in your Excel and name it as you wish.

How To Attach Excel Files and Photos

Step 1: On the home page of Office 365, there will be a navigation bar on the top. This navigation bar has three options in it. In this step,

Step 2: Click on 'Mail' and then click on 'More' option. Click on 'Open a new message' on the next page.

Step 3: Click on 'File' and select 'Attach files'. You can select either an existing file or an email address and select the file you would like to attach. On the next screen, you can add a caption to the file.

Step 4: Click on 'Attach'.

Note: There is no option to attach photos with emails using Office

365. You can, however, upload photos to OneDrive, OneNote, SharePoint and many other cloud-based services, and share them with your contacts.

How To Attach Documents and Spreadsheet

First, you need to open the Microsoft Office 365 Online. When you have logged in, you'll see the following screen. Click on the New button and then click on the + icon.

Click on the Add Documents button.

A new screen will be displayed. To add a document, click on the Browse button and select the document or documents you want to add in the mail.

If you don't want to add all documents, then you can select a file to add and add the selected document.

If you don't have any file, then click on the Add and then select the file type. This will prompt you to select the type of file that you want to add. You can either choose Microsoft Office Word document, Microsoft Office Excel or Microsoft Office PDF. If you choose Microsoft Office Word document, then you'll see different options. You'll see an option to add the document. You can also add a picture to the document. You'll see the option for adding media files as well. You'll also see the option for adding the files to specific folders.

If you don't have any, click on the Files and then you can either browse to the folder where you want to store the file or choose a document to upload. Once the document or document have been uploaded, you can add a media file or a picture.

How To Convert PDFs Into Editable Formats

1. Click on File > New > Document.

2. Enter the name of the document into the template drop down box and select how you want to open the document.

3. Click OK. The Convert button should be grayed out.

4. Click the Convert button.

The document will open in a new window in your browser.

Onceyouaredonewiththeconversion,youcandeletethe document.

If you don't want to delete it, go to the file and change the settings to save it in a different location.

CHAPTER TWELVE

How To Set Up Outlook

After login in to Office 365 website, you will find it as Home page. Now go to "Sign in". In the top left corner you will find "Sign in with Microsoft account". Click on it.

Now you need to select "Office Account". Enter the email address of the Outlook account. It will send you to verification page, now click on it.

Your outlook account is now synced with Office 365. You can go to Home page to check.

Note: if you need to delete your outlook account or login with your Office 365 email, you need to go to Settings and select

"Email + calenging". After clicking on it, you will see a pop-up window. In the upper-right corner, there is a + icon. You can delete the account or sign-in.

How To Customize Outlook

Step #1: Open Microsoft office web app on your web browser.

Step #2: The outlook browser version is the application that you have installed on your system. You can find the outlook 2019 web app installed in system folder.

Step #3: Log in using your email account to get access to the outlook application. If you don't have an email account on your system, you will need to create a new one.

Step #4: Open the Inbox. You should be able to open your inbox, which is similar to outlook web app.

Step #5: You can choose to import all your contacts to outlook on Microsoft office 365 using this import option.

Step #6: To change the web browser application, you can go to the options.

Step #7: Go to the customize tab.

Step #8: You can go to the add-ons tab and add different extensions.

Step #9: You can go to the settings to enable/disable different plugins for this outlook web browser version.

Step #10: You can go to the download tab and download extensions to customize outlook on Microsoft office 365.

Step #11: You can customize and control how much details should be shown to this outlook on Microsoft office 365 using the privacy tab.

Step #12: You can open and close the mail in the mail box using the mail menu.

Step #13: You can go to the search option in this outlook application to search all your email addresses which you have in the system.

Step #14: You can go to the create new mail box option to create a new mail box. You can go to the delete an account option to delete an account from the outlook application.

Step #15: You can go to the settings to configure this outlook application.

Step #16: You can go to the help option to get more information on outlook on Microsoft office 365.

Step #17: You can go to the exit option to exit the office web application.

CHAPTER THIRTEEN

How To Move from Channel to Chat

The steps are:

Step 1: Click on the "Windows Start Button" or press the "Windows" key on your keyboard.

Step 2: After you open the start menu, click on "Channels and chats" in the "Office" folder.

Step 3: The "channels and chats" menu will open.

Step 4: After you click the blue button in the upper right corner of the menu, the "tab strip" will open.

Step 5: Click on "channels" in the upper tab strip.

Step 6: This will move you back to the channel menu, where you should see "chat" option.

Step 7: Click on "chat" to open the chat.

Step 8: Now you're done.

How To Begin A Private chat

Step 1: Login to your Office 365 account with your Microsoft account.

Step 2: Click the chat icon.

Step 3: If you don't have any chat history with the people you want to chat, the Office 365 app will display the people and organizations you've recently talked to. Click on "Add a contact".

Step 4: Select the people or organization you want to send the private chat and click "Add".

Step 5: Type in the message you want to send and click "Send".

Step 6: Wait for the person to receive your message, and click the message notification to see your chat history.

How To Attach File in Your Message

You can't attach a file to your private chat. The only way to do that is to copy the file to your OneDrive folder, share the file and then send a chat message with a link to that file.

When sharing a file, you'll be able to choose what share types you want to allow. I also like to include an option "Embed this file into an email" and choose my personal email address as the recipient. This will place the file inside an email and allow your recipient to view the file in their email client.

Adding An Emoji to Your Message

To begin with, you need to first navigate to settings, followed by privacy, and then click the Manage your emoji usage.

After that, you need to select the text box in the chat where you would like to add the emojis, and add the emojis or emoticons to that text box.

Note: - You can't directly add emojis in the email or the calendar event in the Microsoft Office 365.

Also, you won't be able to directly add emojis in the online form fields like the forms in Outlook, Office 365 web apps, Outlook web apps, Excel, and PowerPoint.

The emoji you select on a chat appears on other devices that you have enabled for emoji use as well.

That is to say, if you choose an emoji on one device, you will also see that emoji in the chats in all other devices on which you have enabled emoji access.

When you type an emoji in the chat, it will appear on the chat on other devices you have enabled to use emojis, as well.

This is how it works in a nutshell.

But on the list of emojis, there is something called a private emoji.

what is a private emoji?

A private emoji is one where you can include it in your chat, and no one else in the Office 365 community can see it in their chat.

This option is only available in Microsoft Office 365 Groups.

It is available in the top level menu that appears when you hover over the emoji on your chat.

This way, you can add the emoji to your chats in private.

How to add emojis to a group chat?

If you need to include an emoji in your group chat, the steps are straightforward:

Select the emoji you want to include in the group chat.

You can also see a list of your most recently used emojis when you go to the emoticon page of your group chat.

Now, all you need to do is click on the green circle icon at the bottom right-hand corner to the right of the emoji.

This will take you to the group's chat, where you can access the emoji.

There is an option on the chat to set it as private and invite your group members.

So, in such a scenario, the only people who can see the emoji in the chat will be you and the people that you are part of the chat with.

Adding Stickers to Your Message

You can find the conversation tab on the left-hand navigation of Office 365. In the navigation menu, click on the conversation button. You will see two options in the menu. The first one is the conversation part and the second one is the thread. Click on the conversation tab. Now, on the left-hand side, click on the conversation. This is the main area of your conversation.

Let's say that you want to add stickers to the conversation, click on the stickers icon. Here you can see all the stickers which are available to you. In order to add the stickers to your conversation, click on the option which you want to add.

Now, go to the body part, and you will see the option to add stickers to the conversation.

To add stickers to your conversation, click on the stickers icon and then go to the body part.

This is how you can add stickers to your conversation.

Now, you can see how you can use the stickers in your conversations. You can save these stickers for future use and you don't have to share the same stickers each time. This is really awesome and helpful feature.

CHAPTER FOURTEEN

Task Overview

The term "task" is used in a number of contexts in SharePoint Online, most commonly referring to task lists.

When a task is created, SharePoint automatically assigns a title and starts saving the user's task on a task list. The user can share a link in the task list with a variety of people. The task list then shows up in their Outlook or OneDrive email.

There are two ways for a task list to appear in the user's Outlook email:

A single task appears, usually with a subject and body. A collection of tasks appears.

In each case, the user who created the task can add people to the list so they can be notified of changes to the task.

You can also define custom fields for a task, which then show up as options in a dropdown when the task is viewed in the task list.

Security Overview

The security in Office 365 is split into two parts: protection of data and protection of communications.

The security of Office 365 is designed to protect data. This means that access to all data and services is controlled by a Microsoft server, not by the user. The Microsoft server will grant access to users and groups as it wants to protect the data. This is more secure than giving the user complete access to all data.

The security of Office 365 is designed to protect communications. This means that communications with Office 365 are protected. This includes communications to and from Office 365, and communications with users in Office 365. This is to protect any information that you send to Office 365 users. Office 365 provides communication security because all data is encrypted by default.

The communications in Office 365 are encrypted by default. This includes the communications between the user and the user's Office 365 server. This is to protect the communications that the user sends to Office 365. There are also protocols to protect the communication from any other type of attack, but they are not encrypted by default.

The data protection in Office 365 is to protect the data against an attack by a third party. This protects the data by encrypting all data on the Internet. The data is stored in the data center, not in a single physical location.

The communications protection in Office 365 is to protect the communications. This protects against any attack on the communications. This includes any attack on the protocols of the protocols of communications. This also includes the communications from the user to the server. This means that the communications between the user and the Office 365 server will be protected.

The user can configure which data is encrypted. The user can also change the encryption level. The user can also use certificates, tokens, or passphrases for all data, or only the data with specific keywords. The user can also configure all data to be stored in the data center, or not at all.

The user cannot change the data. The data will not be encrypted.

The encryption of the communications is not done by the user. The user does not choose which protocols are encrypted, or the level of encryption. Microsoft only encrypts the protocol using Transport Layer Security (TLS). This is done by the Microsoft Office 365 server. The level of encryption depends on the type of data. This can be in transit (encryption of the communications in transit), end to end (encryption between the user and the server), or locally (data that is stored on the local machine).

The data on the cloud is encrypted. This is because the server encrypts the data. The user does not encrypt the data. The data is not protected when stored on the local machine of the user. The user can choose whether to encrypt the data when it is stored.

The user can encrypt data that has not been encrypted on the server. The user can also encrypt data before it is stored on the server. The data will not be encrypted when it is stored on the local machine of the user.

The different types of Microsoft Plans and Their

Features

They aimed the individual subscription at the average person and costs just $8.25 per month. For example, it can cost more if you choose an Office 365 Business Premium plan which includes

50GB of online storage and email archiving. Business Premium costs $11.25 per user per month.

The other two plans are targeted at businesses and organizations with varying requirements.

Office 365 Small Business

The Office 365 Small Business package costs $5 per user per month or $5 per device. It includes the Word, Excel, PowerPoint and OneNote apps and it also includes 1TB of online storage and 1GB of email storage.

Office 365 Education

Office 365 Education is aimed at schools, universities and colleges. The packages are based on a user's needs and cost $11.25 per user per month. There is a 50GB online storage option, so it will enable teachers to back up their files.

The Education Pack also includes Word, Excel and PowerPoint apps and allows you to install apps from the Microsoft Store.

If you are looking for the ultimate productivity package, Office 365 Enterprise E3 for business comes with unlimited remote desktop access to a PC or Mac, and enterprise email addresses for all employees.

Office 365 Enterprise E3 for Business costs $10 per user per month and comes with Office ProPlus apps, an entire suite of business-only productivity tools, such as OneNote, Visio and more.

CHAPTER FIFTEEN

How To Resolve Wrong User I.D

Sign out of the website (if you're not already logged in)

Log in as "user@abcd.com" in the website

Open the Office 365 app, on your phone, and click on your profile picture

Click on "Account" in the menu

Click on "Manage Profile and Services" Switch to "Sign-In & security"

Click on "Update ID" and choose "Get a new ID"

Once the new ID is generated, you will need to contact your customer service provider and provide your new email address.

(I'm not sure if they will charge you anything for this, so it may take a few hours for them to activate the new ID).

How To Decorate A Page With Border

You could make a shape object in Microsoft PowerPoint and place it in the background with no fill. Create a page break on that shape object if you want it to have a title.

In Office 365, go to File > Page Layout > Create a Page Layout, then click the down arrow and choose Page Type > Border and Header. Enter the color you want, thickness, etc.

How To Assign Number to Pages

Each page contains multiple paragraphs of text. Each paragraph is enclosed within a paragraph element. Simply right click on the paragraph element and select Properties and scroll to the Paragraph formatting tab. There you'll see a number indicator just above the first character of the paragraph. You can change the appearance of this number by changing the Font properties, size or color. You can add a border or background to the number by selecting the Number section and then checking the "Show Number". You can also click the number and type a new number.

How To Insert Header to Pages

Go to the beginning of the document. Insert Page Header on top of page footer and set it to start at every page.

Printed by Libri Plureos GmbH in Hamburg,
Germany

9 798330 677320